GREECE

EUROPE

**BC
2000**

2000-1900 Greek-speaking tribes arrive

2000 Stonehenge built in Britain

1650-1450 Mycenaeans grow in power

1500-1300 Bronze Age in northern Europe

1450 Cretan civilization destroyed

1220? Troy destroyed by expedition from mainland Greece

1150

1150 Dorians invade Greece. Collapse of Mycenaean civilization

1100s Phoenician colonies in Spain

900-750 Rise of city-states

900 Rise of Etruscans in Italy

776 Traditional date of first Olympic Games

750 Homer's Iliad and Odyssey composed

753 Traditional date of founding of Rome

700-500 Sparta dominates Peloponnese

600 Greeks found city of Massilia (now Marseilles) in France

507

507 Athenian democracy begins

509 Roman nobles drive out their Etruscan kings

490-479 Persian Wars

490 Common people of Rome rebel against nobles. They win some rights

477-405 Athens dominates the Aegean, and enjoys its Golden Age

450 Celtic La Tène culture develops

431-404 Peloponnesian War between Athens and Sparta

380 Celts attack Rome

356-338 Philip of Macedon makes himself master of Greece

336 Philip is murdered and his son Alexander succeeds him

336-323 Alexander wins an empire stretching from Egypt to north India

323

323 Alexander dies aged 32

NEAR EAST

EAST ASIA

**BC
2000**

**2372-2255 Akkadian empire; founded by
Sargon**

2040-1633 Egypt's Middle Kingdom

1792-1750 Hammurabi rules Babylon

1567-1085 Egypt's New Kingdom

1450-1180 Hittite empire at its height

**1200 Sea Peoples raid Mediterranean
coasts**

**1150 Greeks begin to colonize coast of
Asia Minor**

973 Solomon becomes King of Israel

**2500 Indus Valley civilization arises in
India**

**1500 Indus Valley civilization falls to
invaders**

1500-1027 Shang dynasty in China

1150

1027-256 Chou dynasty in China

**587 Nebuchadrezzar of Babylon besieges
Jerusalem**

539 Persians conquer Babylonia

**c 600 Early cities near river Ganges in
India**

563 Birth of the Buddha in India

551 Chinese sage Confucius born

533 Persians invade India

507

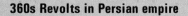

360s Revolts in Persian empire

**334-332 Alexander the Great conquers the
Persian empire**

**326 Alexander the Great invades north
India**

323

Ancient Greece

WARWICK PRESS

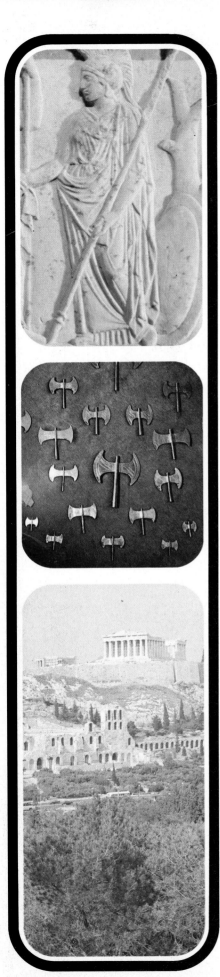

Contents

Top: The goddess Athene, shown wearing her helmet as goddess of victory. Center: Part of a hoard of golden double axes found in Crete. These axes clearly were sacred to the Minoans. Bottom: The Parthenon stands on top of the Acropolis in Athens.

Editorial

Author
Christopher Fagg B.A.

Editor
Frances M. Clapham

Illustrators
Constance and Brian Dear
Peter Connolly
Richard Hook

Published 1979 by Warwick Press, 730 Fifth Avenue, New York, New York 10019.

First published in Great Britain by Longman Group, Limited, 1978.

Copyright © 1978 by Grisewood & Dempsey Ltd.

Printed in Italy by New Interlitho, Milan.

6 5 4 3 2 1   All rights reserved

Library of Congress Catalog Card No. 78-68532

ISBN 0-531-09124-4

Ancient Greece

Life was hard for the ancient Greeks. Their cities were huddled on little pockets of fertile coastland. Finding food became a problem as they grew. They were cut off from one another by rugged mountains. But it was the Greeks who developed the first civilization in Europe.

Our knowledge of ancient Greece centers on Athens. Here many of the most beautiful of all the buildings and sculptures in ancient Greece were built. Here democracy – that form of government in which all citizens have a share – grew up. And Athens was certainly one of the most powerful cities in Greece. But there were other states that played as great a part. To the south was Sparta that produced the finest and bravest soldiers of the time. Across the Aegean Sea were the many rich Greek colonies. In them Greek writing and literature, medicine and science had their beginnings.

The Greeks were a proud people. The city states were constantly at war with one another. For the Greeks were not united by a common rule. Instead they were linked by a common culture. They shared the same gods, the same language and way of life. This book looks at the civilization that Greeks developed – a civilization which, more than any other, has shaped our world today.

Above: Corinth was famous for its brightly painted pottery. The animals on this vessel show the influence of Eastern art. Below: A pottery model of women making bread, from Thebes in Boeotia.

The Glory That Was Greece

The civilization which grew up in Greece spread all through the Mediterranean. ''The Glory that was Greece'', as Edgar Allan Poe described it, has inspired scholars and artists for countless generations.

The ancient Greeks played more part in shaping our lives today than any other ancient people. Their poetry, sculpture, drama, philosophy and science have all influenced the development of our modern world. Who were the Greeks, and how did they live?

The first Greeks were herdsmen who arrived in the mountainous peninsula of Greece about 2000 BC. They settled in villages on the narrow coastal plains and came into contact with traders from the island of Crete. Over the centuries the mainland Greeks – the Mycenaeans – took up many of the Cretan ways of life. After Crete was devastated by earthquakes, the Mycenaeans took control of the island. But this magnificent civilization was destroyed by new waves of Greek-speaking invaders, the Dorians.

After a time of chaos and confusion, a new Greek civilization

Athenians lead a heifer to the sacrifice. This is a scene from the great frieze which decorated the Parthenon. The frieze, 175 yards (160 meters) long, shows the Great Panathenea, a magnificent celebration held every fourth year.

CHRONOLOGY

2600–2000 BC	Growth of pre-Greece civilization in Crete.
2000–1700	Greek speaking tribes arrive in Greece. First palaces built in Crete, destroyed about 1700.
1650–1450	New palaces in Crete. Mycenaean Greeks start to grow in power in fortified palaces in mainland Greece.
1450 (approx.)	Palaces in Crete destroyed by earthquakes. Mycenaean Greeks invade Crete and occupy the palace at Knossos.
1375	Palace at Knossos destroyed.
1189	Force of Mycenaean Greeks attack and destroy city of Troy in Asia Minor.
1100–900	Dorians (warlike tribes speaking a form of Greek) invade Greece. Collapse of Mycenaean civilization. Refugees from invasions flee and found cities on coast of Asia Minor and eastern Aegean islands.
900–750	City life develops. Growth of trade between Asiatic (eastern) Greeks and mainland cities, especially Corinth. City populations grow. Surplus population from many cities emigrates to found colonies in Sicily, south Italy and Asia Minor.
800 (approx.)	Homer's *Iliad* and *Odyssey* composed.
800–700	Writing introduced from the east, spreads quickly over Greek world.
776	Olympic Games started at Elis, in southern Greece.
720	Sparta expands into Peloponnese (the southern peninsula of Greece). Spartans take over the fertile lands of the Messenians.
705	Hesiod writes *Works and Days*.
700–600	Athenians get rid of their kings. Tyrants rule in Corinth, Megara, Sicyon.
546	Persian empire takes over eastern Greek cities.
510	With the aid of Sparta, tyrants are driven out of Athens.
507	Athenian democracy begins under Cleisthenes.
490	First Persian invasion of Greece. Battle of Marathon, Persians defeated by Athens.
480	Second Persian invasion defeated by united Greek fleet at battle of Salamis.
479	Remnants of Persian army defeated at battle of Plataea.
475–450	Build-up of Athenian empire: 265 cities pay tribute to Athens.
422	Pericles leads Athens in its Golden Age.
431–404	Peloponnesian War between Sparta and Athens.
429	Death of Pericles.
415	Disastrous defeat of Athenian expedition sent to conquer Syracuse, in Sicily.
404	Surrender of Athens. Spartans control Greece.
371	Thebes, under Epaminondas, defeat Spartans at battle of Leuctra.
358–338	Rise of Macedonia under King Philip.
338	Philip makes himself master of Greece at battle of Chaironeia.
336	Philip assassinated, his son Alexander becomes king.
334–323	Alexander the Great invades Persian empire at the head of a Greek army, eventually conquering an empire stretching from Egypt to India.
323	Alexander dies at Babylon, aged 32.
323–280	Struggles between Alexander's generals result in break-up of his empire into three parts—Macedonia, Asia Minor, and Egypt.
280–197	Attempts by old Greek city-states to throw off control of Macedonia. Eventually, Romans back Greeks and defeat Macedonia at battle of Cynoscephalae (197 BC).
146	Greek cities rise against domination of Rome. They are defeated at the battle of Corinth.
145	Rome finally combines Greek cities into province of Macedonia.

grew up. It was a world of small city states which made a living from trade. Although they were widely scattered, they shared the same language and traditions. Just because they were isolated, the cities held on to their Greek ways of life all the more strongly. Greek religious festivals drew pilgrims together from every part of the Greek world.

The cities competed with one another for land, for trade, and for glory. Each tried to build the most magnificent temples and attract the best teachers and thinkers. Architects and artists, scientists, doctors, and philosophers traveled from one city to another. In this way Greek knowledge spread widely around the Mediterranean, and even into Persia. In the end the rivalries between the Greek cities flared into bitter warfare. This came to an end only when Alexander the Great conquered Greece.

Alexander united a Greek army and led it against the Persians. He became master of the greatest empire the world had ever known. After his death his empire was split up. But the Greek world went on, even after Rome took over, two centuries later. Greek was still the language of educated people all over the Mediterranean, and Greek scholars were in great demand in Rome itself. Many of the great Greek sculptures are known to us only from copies made by the admiring Romans. Some of the Greek ideas on arts and sciences survived for more than a thousand years. They became the starting point for our modern thought.

Above: A vase showing Jason and his wife, the sorceress Medea, sacrificing a ram. The most famous legend about Jason tells how he sailed the Argo with a crew of other heroes to capture the Golden Fleece.

Below: This map shows Greece and its principal colonies. There were many rich and powerful Greek cities all round the Mediterranean and on the Black Sea coasts.

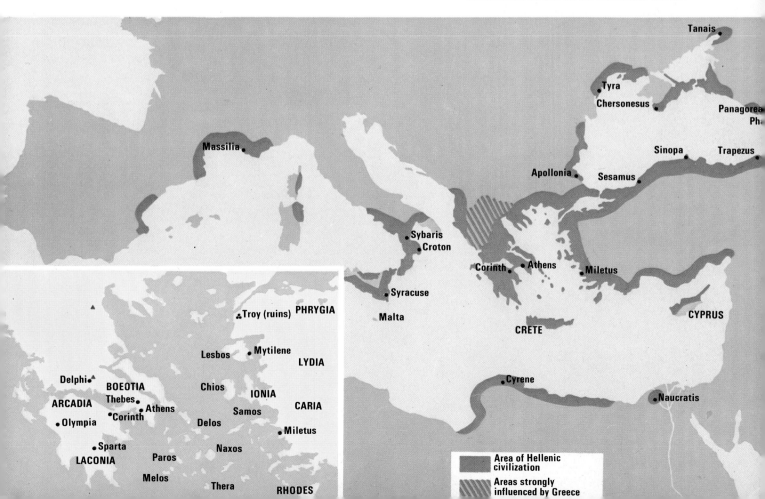

Tanais

Tyra
Chersonesus
Panagorea
Ph.

Massilia

Sinopa
Trapezus

Apollonia
Sesamus

Sybaris
Croton

Corinth • Athens
Miletus

Syracuse

Malta

CYPRUS

CRETE

Troy (ruins)   PHRYGIA

Lesbos • Mytilene
LYDIA

Delphi

BOEOTIA   Chios
Thebes   IONIA
ARCADIA   CARIA
        • Athens   Samos
• Corinth
        Delos
• Olympia   • Miletus

Cyrene

Naucratis

• Sparta
LACONIA   Paros   Naxos

Melos

Thera   RHODES

Area of Hellenic civilization

Areas strongly influenced by Greece

Kingdom of Minos

Nearly four thousand years ago a great and luxurious civilization flourished on the island of Crete. Who were its inhabitants, and why did their peaceful way of life come to an end?

The legend of Theseus was a favorite of the ancient Greeks. It told how, long ago, the island of Crete in the Aegean Sea was ruled by the great King Minos. Every seven years Minos demanded a tribute from Athens of seven young men and seven girls as a sacrifice to the terrible Minotaur. The Minotaur was half man and half bull, and lived beneath Minos's vast palace. Theseus, son of the king of Athens, was determined to end this cruel tribute. He sailed with the victims for Crete. Helped by Minos's daughter Ariadne, he found his way through the labyrinth in which the Minotaur lived, killed it, and escaped with his companions. Later he became King of Athens.

Even as they told the story, most Athenians probably thought it was just a legend. And so it remained until 1899, when the British archeologist Arthur Evans began to excavate at Knossos in Crete. What he found amazed scholars everywhere – gold, silver,

Below: The palace of Knossos at its height. It was a vast area of storehouses, workshops, state apartments, living quarters, and offices. It had an excellent piped water supply and an equally good drainage system. The important rooms were decorated with frescoes. Some of the buildings were crowned with curiously shaped stones that Evans was convinced were bulls' horns.

elaborate buildings with fantastically painted walls. These were the remains of a civilization that had existed long before the earliest known Greeks. The legend of Theseus had, after all, been based on history.

The Minoans (as Arthur Evans called them after King Minos) lived a life of peace and comfort. The rich soil provided good grazing for sheep and goats. Farmers could grow far more than they needed. Wine and raisins, olives and olive oil were traded in Egypt and the Aegean area in return for gold and silver, copper and alabaster.

Many of the Minoans lived in villages and small towns, while landowners had large houses on their estates. Most important of all were the great palaces like that at Knossos. Here rich people lived in luxury, in large and airy rooms decorated with pictures of fabulous beasts, flowers, or sea creatures. Small paintings show elegant ladies and men with curled hair. They wore beautiful jewelry and used delicately painted pottery, made by the craftsmen whose workshops surrounded the palace. Like other Cretan palaces, Knossos was built round a central court. The official rooms were on the upper stories. Domestic quarters lower down were built around light-wells, which kept out the cold winter winds and the burning summer sun. Within the palace itself were many storerooms; 220,000 gallons (about 1 million liters) of olive oil could be stored there. But none of the palaces had strong walls for defense.

We do not know what brought this great civilization to an end. But in 1450 BC some catastrophe occurred – perhaps an earthquake or an invasion. Towns and palaces were burned and abandoned. Knossos alone remained, and it was lived in by Mycenaeans from mainland Greece. In 1375 Knossos itself burned down. The only clue to this final disaster is marks on the walls, showing that a south wind was blowing as it burned.

A bronze figure of a bull with an athlete leaping from its horns.

THE BULL AND THE SNAKE

As he excavated Knossos, Evans found many paintings and statues showing bulls. Some showed a bull charging, and some showed a youth somersaulting over the bull's back. These works of art suggest a form of "bull-dancing" in which boys and girls seized the bull's horns and then sprang over its back.

The bull was clearly very important to the Minoans. Knossos has suffered many earthquakes, which can produce roaring sounds like those of an angry bull. Perhaps the Minoans felt that there was a bull-god beneath the ground.

The Minoans probably worshiped a mother-goddess. Rings and statuettes show either a priestess or the goddess herself, with snakes twined round her arms.

This scene from a painted stone sarcophagus from Crete shows an altar on which lies a bull. To the right, a woman lays offerings on another altar.

The Mycenaeans

The poems of Homer told of ancient warrior kings who lived in fortresses and owned vast treasures of gold. Now we know that these people really existed.

Above: The walls of the citadel at Tiryns, at the head of the Gulf of Argos in the Pelopponese. The immensely thick walls are built of huge blocks of stone. Later generations of Greeks were sure that such vast fortifications could only have been built by giants. Within the walls at Tiryns lies a palace, in which archeologists have discovered wall-paintings in the Minoan style. Among other subjects they show the kind of bull-leaping rituals also seen at Knossos, in Crete.

Homer's great poem the *Iliad* describes how the city of Troy was besieged by a Greek army led by King Agamemnon of Mycenae, a city "rich in gold". Until the end of the 19th century people thought that the warriors Homer described must be only legendary. They did not correspond to what was known of the early Greeks. But then archeologists discovered the remains of an earlier Greek civilization – a civilization of warriors who lived in luxury and who buried their dead with staggering treasures of gold. In many ways these warriors resembled the people Homer had written about. Their civilization is known as Mycenaean, after one of its most important citadels.

The Mycenaeans swept down into Greece from the plains of Russia in about 2000 BC, driving before them their herds of cattle. They learned from the farming peoples they conquered how to cultivate vines and olives, and how to sail. This was important, because the mountainous country made it easier to sail around the coast than to travel overland.

Mycenaean settlements grew up around the coast. Each settlement had a heavily fortified citadel. Beneath its walls was a straggling group of houses, and beyond that fields and pastures. The chief lived in a building called a *megaron*, which had a pillared entrance, an antechamber, and a hall with a great central hearth. At Pylos the hall was almost 50 feet (15 meters) long. The floor was plastered and painted in geometric patterns, and on the wall behind the throne was a painting of lions and griffins,

HOMER, THE BLIND POET

The poet Homer was born, some time before 800 BC, on the island of Chios in the Aegean Sea. We know almost nothing of his life, for even in the 6th century he had become almost as much of a legend as the gods and heroes of his poems. All that can be said is that he traveled widely, and that he became blind.

Homer's two poems *The Iliad* and *The Odyssey* live on 3000 years later. *The Iliad* tells of the siege and destruction of the city of Troy by the Greeks led by Agamemnon. *The Odyssey* describes the wandering of one of the Greek besiegers, King Odysseus of Ithaca, on his journey home after Troy had fallen.

Homer's characters are very human. They are fierce and warlike, brave and chivalrous. Sometimes they are petty and quarrelsome. But they are quick to recognize courage and nobility, even in their enemies. Homer's poetry was known and loved throughout the cities of the Greek world.

This vase shows the destruction of Troy. The Trojan king, Priam, lies on the ground about to be killed by a Greek warrior. Menelaus is prevented from harming his wife Helen by the goddess Aphrodite.

imaginary animals with the head and wings of an eagle and the body of a lion. Around the megaron were kitchens, storerooms, and women's rooms.

Life in Mycenaean times was one of constant skirmish, if not actual warfare. Chiefs led their people on raiding parties. Nobles were kept fully occupied in the search for plunder and for glory. The citadels were fortified with walls of vast stone blocks. Staircases were built within the walls so that hidden water supplies could be reached in a siege.

The Mycenaeans reached the height of their power after the decline of Crete. But about 1200 BC came a new wave of invaders, the Dorians. They had weapons of iron, far superior to the bronze of the Mycenaeans. Within a hundred years all the Mycenaean strongholds had fallen.

Discoveries at Mycenae. Left: The head of a female idol of painted clay, 12 inches (30 centimeters) high. It dates from very early farming settlements. Above: A beaten gold mask, wrongly identified by Schliemann as the funeral mask of Agamemnon.

Below: A fragment of wall painting – showing three donkey-headed demons.

DISCIPLE OF HOMER

Heinrich Schliemann was born in 1826, the son of a German pastor. When he was a small boy he learned the story of Troy; and he made up his mind that one day he would find the city. At 14 he started work as a grocer's boy. By the time he was 36 he was a millionaire. In 1868 he set out to look for Troy.

Schliemann decided to look for Troy not on its traditional site but on a small hill some distance away. Within a short time he had uncovered the remains of nine cities, each built on the ruins of the one before. And he found a vast treasure.

Next Schliemann turned to mainland Greece, to the site of ancient Mycenae. This was described by Homer as the city of Agamemnon. Within the massive stone walls of the old citadel, he found a ring of graves. In them were human remains surrounded by a glittering treasure. Schliemann's imagination was fired by a gold mask, showing a bearded face. He sent a telegram to the king of Greece, claiming: "I have looked on the face of Agamemnon."

Schliemann was wrong. These graves were later found to be some 300 years older than the Trojan War.

Gods, Myths, and Legends

The many gods and goddesses of Greece played an important part in everyday life. For the Greeks not only looked to them for advice on all important matters, but believed that the gods could intervene in human affairs.

This magnificent bronze statue, over 7 feet (2·5 meters) high, was found on the sea-bed near Cape Artemisium, Greece. Dating from about 450 BC, it shows Zeus, or perhaps his brother, Poseidon, in the act of hurling a weapon – now lost. The figure shows very clearly how the Greeks thought of their gods – as physically perfect human beings.

cruel, loyal or jealous, peaceful or violent. But their supreme power allowed them to be independent of mankind.

A Greek approached his gods in the same way as he might approach a powerful earthly king. Respectfully, he would offer presents (the sacrifice), showing by his words that he was aware of the god's power. Then he would make his request, reminding the god of other offerings made in the past.

This was the correct form for prayers to the gods. It was very often used, for the Greeks were a deeply religious – even superstitious – people. There was a vast number of temples, shrines, sanctuaries, and altars all over the Greek world.

But respect is not fear. The Greeks did not grovel before their gods. When they sacrificed an animal they offered only the god's due proportion of it – usually a tenth. The rest they ate themselves. The offering was an act of hospitality; and it showed that the Greeks thought the gods appreciated courtesy and generosity.

The Greeks thought their gods lived in a large family in a land beyond the clouds that gather over the high peak of Mount Olympus. Ruled by their king, Zeus, they were immortal beings who controlled the weather, the growth of crops, and earthquakes, as well as the movements of the Sun, the Moon, and the stars.

Yet the Greeks did not regard their gods as cold, faraway forces with no interest in human affairs. Their gods looked like humans, and had human faults and virtues. They could be kind or

Legends and heroes

The Greeks were a proud people. They had a vast store of legends about their beginnings and their history. These explained how their gods came into being and how the cities they lived in were founded. In legends, too, the Greeks kept alive the memory of famous ancestors.

With many thousands of stories, the Greeks invented a host of legendary beings. Every region, every mountain, even every spring and cave had its own tale of gods and heroes.

KINGS OF THE GODS

The 8th-century poet Hesiod told many legends of the gods. He tells how Zeus was the son of Mother Earth and had two brothers, Poseidon and Hades. Together they rebelled against the older gods, and cast them out. Zeus became lord of heaven and earth, Poseidon became god of the sea, and Hades became king of the Underworld and ruled over the ghosts of the dead. Zeus married the goddess of childbirth, Hera, and set about founding the family of the gods.

Right: Athene is born from the forehead of Zeus — the result of a blow from the hammer of Hephaestus to cure Zeus's headache.

THE FOUNDATION OF ATHENS

Athens always prided itself as being the oldest of the Greek cities. The legend of its foundation told how the first king of Attica, Cecrops, asked for a divine protector for the city. A quarrel arose between Athene and Poseidon as to which one of them it should be. A contest was decided on. First Poseidon struck the ground with his trident and out gushed a spring of water. Then Athene struck the ground with her spear, and an olive tree emerged, laden with fruit. Athene's olive tree, which was to bring the city its wealth, was judged the winner; and so the new city got its name.

Left: Athene and Hera, the wife of Zeus. Athene is always shown armed with helmet, spear, and shield.
Below: Heracles (Hercules) fighting a monster. He is dressed in the skin of the Nemean lion, which he killed in the first of his 12 Labors for King Eurystheus of Argos.

THE HEROES

The Greek heroes included men like Jason of Thessaly, Theseus of Athens, Heracles of Thebes, Perseus of Argos, and Odysseus of Ithaca. A hero was a man who was brave and chivalrous. Such men fought monsters, made epic sea-voyages, won mighty victories, and performed impossible tasks. Once a hero had given his word he fulfilled it, whatever the cost.

The Greeks saw a hero's actions as the nearest that mortal man could get to the perfection of the gods.

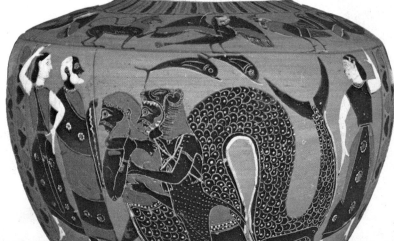

A bronze head of Apollo. He was god of the arts that made men civilized, and the plagues that destroyed them.

Poseidon: The god of the sea, of tidal waves, and of earthquakes. He was often represented as having the tail of a fish, and armed with a trident. As Poseidon-Hippios, he also ruled horses.

Hades: The ruler of the gloomy Underworld, where the souls of the dead lived.

Hera: The goddess of marriage and childbirth. She was the wife of Zeus, and many of the stories about her tell of her constant nagging and jealousy.

Athene: The goddess of wisdom and courage. She was born fully formed from Zeus's forehead, armed with her spear, helmet, and shield. She was worshiped in a number of roles, among them Athene Nike, goddess of victory, and Athene Ergane, goddess of cunning.

Dionysus: The god of wine and intoxication. The son of Zeus, Dionysus incurred the hatred of Hera, who tried to kill him. Everywhere he went, he and his band of wild followers established vine-growning. In return, people wor-

Hermes, messenger of the gods, holding his wand of office. From the Temple of Artemis at Ephesus.

shiped him as a god, celebrating his festivals with drunken parties.

Apollo: The god of poetry and the arts, but also the healer and the sender of plagues. The son of Zeus, Apollo and his sister Artemis were born on the sacred island of Delos. At Delphi, Apollo killed the serpent Python, which Hera had sent to destroy him. There he was worshiped as Apollo Pythia, god of prophecy. Because he sent plagues to kill men he was also thought to be able to cure them, so he became the god of medicine and purification.

Zeus: The king of the Olympian gods. He ruled the weather, especially thunderstorms, and was usually shown armed with a thunderbolt. In some places, he was also worshiped as the patron god of guests and the home. The eagle was his sacred bird.

Bronze head of Aphrodite by Praxitiles, the greatest sculptor of the 4th century BC.

THE NATURE SPIRITS

Country people in Greece had a great many beliefs dating from earliest times. They believed in nature gods like Pan — the god of deep forests and remote mountain tops. Pan had the body of a man, with the legs and tail of a goat. Goat's horns grew from his forehead. He was usually pictured playing a simple shepherd's pipe made of reeds bound together.

A 4th-century BC mirror-cover. It shows Aphrodite playing at dice with Pan, watched by Eros (Cupid).

SACRED SITES

The Mediterranean lands were inhabited for at least a thousand years before the Greeks arrived. Naturally there were stories about this or that place that went back farther than anyone could remember. For the Greeks, the mere fact that there were many legends about a particular spot was enough to make it a holy place, and they added stories of their own gods. In this way places like Delphi, Eleusis, Dodona, and the island of Delos became very important for the Greeks. They were thought so sacred that they could not be involved in any war.

Delphi and Delos, two of the most important sites, were both sacred to Apollo. Delos was his birthplace, and at Delphi he slew the serpent Python. This became the chief seat of his cult, where he spoke through his priestess, the Pythia. Her ravings were studied by priests who gave them as answers to people who had come to consult the oracle.

Delphi was a place where many people came to find out about the future from an oracle. It was therefore in a good position to hear the latest news from the whole of the Greek world. So the advice its priests gave was based on sound and up-to-date information — which was rare in a world of scattered communities. But the oracle's reputation was safeguarded by answers that could be read in different ways.

Above: A stone lion on the tiny island of Delos, one of nine lions dedicated to the goddess Leto. Delos had shrines to Apollo, Artemis, and Hera. Below: The ruins of the Temple of Apollo at Delphi. Below left: The Omphalos stone, placed in Delphi to mark the navel of the world.

City States

Ancient Greece was not a united state. It was a collection of individual cities, each with its surrounding farmland.

The strong citadels of the Mycenaeans could not stand up against the fierce invaders from the north. Almost all of them were destroyed around 1200 BC and it was 200 years before Greek cities flourished again. But these new cities were built on much the same lines as the old. Each had its fortified citadel, the *acropolis*, on a piece of high ground. At its foot was the *astu*, a group of houses in which the townsfolk lived. Around the city was a pocket of fertile land where enough food could be grown to feed its inhabitants.

The barren, mountainous countryside made travel overland slow and difficult, so most of the cities were built near the sea. But sea travel was often hazardous, too, so these little states were rather isolated. Partly because of this they were quite separate. Although they sometimes joined together briefly against a common enemy, the history of Greece is completely overshadowed by the wars between the states. Two of the most powerful were Athens and Sparta.

At first the states were ruled by kings, advised by a council of land-owning nobles. But in nearly all of them the power of the king quickly declined, until he became no more than another noble.

Soon the Greek islanders began to trade across the sea to the mainland. In cities like Corinth, Thebes, and Athens a new class of person arose whose money came from trade and industry. These people began to rival the old nobility. Their power was not based on birth and land. In some cities they seized power in the name of the people.

From the beginning of the 5th century, Athenian pottery was an important export. Potters painted their wares with every kind of scene, from the stories of Homer to details of daily life. This 6th-century black-figure bowl shows an Athenian potter working on a krater – a kind of mixing-bowl. It stands on a heavy wheel, probably turned by an assistant.

A 5th-century Athenian red-figure bowl showing a cobbler at work in his shop. Completed shoes hang on the wall above his head.

An enormous amount of Greek pottery has survived — some whole but much of it in pieces. In Greece there were large deposits of clay. Greek potters made pots and pans, oil lamps, water jars and roof tiles, commercial storage jars, and so on. Much of what they made was plain and simple, but they also produced beautifully decorated and delicate wine cups and jugs.

Among the cities making this kind of decorated pottery from the 7th century on were Athens and Corinth. Corinth was a major center of trade from the cities of the east. Its potters painted their pots with eastern monsters.

There were two main ways of decorating pottery. The "black-figure" vases (see page 15) and the "red-figure" vases (see page 9) soon became the specialities of Athens. The red was the natural color of the clay.

Left: A selection of Greek pottery vessels. The large amphorae held liquid or grain. The krater was used to mix water and wine. The tiny flask would have held perfume.

AGRICULTURE

In Mycenaean times Greece was a land of thickly forested mountains. Crop-growing and stock-raising were limited to the narrow, winding inland valleys and the strip of coastal plain. A farmer grew a little wheat and barley, and tended olive and fig trees and a few grapevines. He reared pigs and kept a goat for milk and cheese.

By 650 BC things had changed for the worse. The forest had been cut down for ship-timbers, or made into charcoal for metal working. Without tree-roots and fallen leaves to hold them back, the heavy winter rains cascaded down bare mountainsides, stripping off fertile soil. This was disastrous for the peasant farmers; in a bad year they could not even grow enough to feed their own families.

In Athens, the statesman Solon tried to solve the problem by encouraging farmers to replant their land with olive trees. But the deep roots of the olive sucked up moisture from the soil and did nothing to knit the topsoil together. Soon Athens found that it could no longer feed its population. It came to rely completely on grain imported from Egypt and the colonies around the Black Sea.

Top right: This 6th-century vase shows men beating an olive tree with long poles to bring down the ripe fruit.

A 6th-century Doric temple at Agrigento, then a rich colony in southern Sicily. All over the Greek world, temples were built to a simple plan that looked back to the wooden temples of the 9th and 10th centuries BC. The columns of this temple are only imitations in stone of the wooden pillars which supported the thatched roofs of early temples. Although the temples of the 5th century and later were more richly decorated, the basic plan did not change.

LANGUAGE AND LITERATURE

All the Greeks spoke the same language, though there were many different dialects. But until the 8th century they had no form of written language. Then the Eastern Ionian Greeks came into contact with the Phoenicians in a struggle over trade routes. The Phoenicians, who came from coastal cities in the Near East, used a Semitic alphabet something like Hebrew. It had signs for consonants but no vowels. In a great leap forward the Greeks invented signs to represent their vowels, and the written Greek language was born. The alphabet we use today is based very closely on the one that the Greeks developed.

At first the Greeks followed the Phoenician example of writing from right to left. Then they tried a method in which the first line went right to left, but the next left to right. Soon they settled down to writing from left to right.

The earliest Greek literature was poetry. Homer was the last of the poets whose works were handed down in spoken form. His poems were written down within a hundred years or so of his death. His influence was enormous. When Hesiod, a poet-farmer, wrote a book of instruction for farmers called *Works and Days*, he wrote in Homeric verse. Solemn hymns in the style of Homer were composed for great public festivals.

The Colonies

Greek colonies were scattered round the Mediterranean coast, from France to Asia Minor. Many of them grew much richer than the mainland "mother" cities, and they produced great scholars and scientists. They were linked to one another and to the mainland cities by a common language and way of life.

Today Greece means the mainland country and the nearby islands. But in ancient times there were Greek cities as far afield as the Black Sea coast, Sicily, and southern France (see page 9). The first colonists left Greece when the Mycenaeans were defeated by invaders from the north called Dorians. Later colonies were founded because the populations of the city states on the mainland grew so much that they could not be fed from the surrounding farmland.

Colonial expeditions began with a visit to the oracle at Delphi. There the priests were asked for their advice on a good site for a new city, and what the forms of worship there should be. This was particularly important, for no colony could hope to succeed

A Greek colonizing expedition, about 500 BC. The colonists have chosen a site near the sea, below a steep hill on which they will build a fortified citadel. Traders, attracted by the news of a new colony, have drawn their ships up on the beach. The city will be laid out in a grid of broad avenues, and surrounded by the city wall. At the center will be the marketplace (agora), together with temples, law-courts, and council chambers. The new city will be a place of refuge in case of attacks by local barbarian tribes.

without the good will of the gods. When the colonists had chosen their site they bought supplies of seed corn and domestic animals, and chartered ships to take them to their new home. Sometimes they had to subdue the local tribesmen when they arrived.

The new city would be built on the familiar Greek pattern, with a fortified hill or *acropolis*. Within the main city would be the market place or *agora*, and a temple dedicated to the patron god or goddess. Around it would lie good farmland, producing enough to feed the city and with luck to trade back to the hungry mainland. The new city usually kept up close links with the "mother" city from which the colonists had set out. But it was independent and had its own laws and government.

Cities at risk

The earliest Greek cities in Asia Minor were built by refugees from the Dorians. They were sited at the mouths of fertile river valleys and soon became prosperous. But they had one great fault. They were difficult to defend against the powerful empires of Asia. The south of Italy and the island of Sicily, too, were heavily colonized. The Italian and Sicilian Greek cities grew rich and powerful, but finally they fell victim to the power of Rome.

A Greek lived very much the same sort of life in Asia Minor, mainland Greece, the south of France, or the north of Africa. He lived in the same sort of buildings, spoke the same language, and worshiped the same gods. Above all, he had the same customs and traditions. So Greeks all over the Mediterranean region had far more in common with one another than with their non-Greek neighbors.

THE FIRST SCIENTISTS

The first great Greek scientists and philosophers lived on the fertile coasts of Asia Minor. Here life was less of a struggle than on mainland Greece. Men found time to travel widely, and to think about the nature of the world they lived in.

At Miletus in the 6th century BC men like Thales and his pupil Anaximander made discoveries, based on careful observation. Thales made important advances in the practice of surveying and geometry. He was able to reckon the height of the pyramids from the length of their shadows, and he drew up navigation tables for ships. His studies of the stars led him to predict the eclipse of the Sun in May 585 BC. Anaximander made a map of the Earth and constructed sun-dials. He noticed that the shells and skeletons of sea animals were to be found even on high mountains. So he said that the sea had once been much higher and that men themselves had started as sea-creatures.

For the first time scientists looked beyond myths and legends to try to find the truth about the universe.

SHIPS

The wealth of Greek cities depended on trade. Merchant vessels plowed the seas between the islands of the Aegean, or skirted the rugged coasts of eastern Greece. New routes were opened up as colonies were founded in Sicily and southern Italy.

Trading vessels in the Mediterranean were always plagued by pirates, whose fast warships could easily overtake the cumbersome merchant vessels. So the trading nations built warships to protect their merchantmen from pirates. The light, fast warships the Greeks built in the 8th century helped them to gain control of the Eastern Mediterranean from the Phoenician sailors who until then had been in command of the trade routes.

Merchant vessels were sturdy and round, so that they could carry large cargoes. They were powered by sail. The warships were long and thin, with a heavy ram in front with which to sink an enemy. They were powered by oars when attacking, with a sail for cruising around.

Ships had no charts or navigation instruments, and once out of sight of land were in grave danger of getting lost. But the mountainous coasts and islands were visible for many miles.

This early bronze stand (right) from Cyprus shows a man carrying an ingot of metal. The island of Cyprus was the main source for copper.

Warring States

War was commonplace in ancient Greece, when rivalry in trade and for land often led to fights between neighboring states and their allies. But only Sparta kept a professional army; other states called up their citizens.

The small, independent states of mainland Greece were often at war with one another. This was usually because one of them seemed dangerously powerful to its neighbors. They would band together against their common enemy in a short-lived alliance. Of all the states, only Sparta had a permanent army; the others raised one only in time of war.

This meant that Sparta was the most powerful military force in Greece, and a sought-after ally. But Spartans were difficult allies. On a number of occasions they turned up late for battles because they had been occupied with festivals.

A Greek army was made up of cavalry (drawn from the wealthy) and *hoplites* or heavy infantry (of ordinary citizens). The hoplites fought in a formation called the phalanx, arranged in ranks one behind the other. The usual tactic was to walk towards the enemy and then charge, hoping to scatter the opposing force by sheer weight of numbers. If this failed, the fighting broke up into hand-to-hand combats until one side or the other could withdraw for long enough to re-form. The Spartans walked up to the enemy at a steady pace to the sound of flutes and then refused to retreat.

A 6th-century BC bowl showing a merchant ship (left) and warship at sea.

THE WOODEN WALL

"The Athenians will defend their city with a wall of wood" said the oracle when Xerxes of Persia threatened Athens in 480 BC. What did this mean? The Athenian statesman Themistocles was in no doubt: the "wall of wood" was made up of Athens's fighting ships. Themistocles knew how important sea-power was to Athens. Even if an enemy occupied the country around, supplies could be brought in by sea. When Athens discovered a rich silver mine in 483, he persuaded the council to build ships. Within two years 100 triremes had been built.

An Athenian plate showing a Scythian archer. Only in the 4th century did Greek generals use light troops such as archers and slingers (peltasts). They were used to protect the flank of the heavy infantry, or to hold off an enemy while the foot-soldiers re-formed their positions.

THE PERSIAN WARS

In 521 BC Darius I came to the throne of the wealthy Persian Empire. It controlled the Greek cities of Asia Minor. In 499 the Asian Greeks rebelled, calling on mainland Greece for help. Only Athens and Eretria answered the call. The revolt was soon crushed, but Darius decided to punish Athens. In 490 Darius landed in Greece but was defeated at Marathon. Ten years later his successor Xerxes tried again, and the Persians were finally defeated.

Marathon, 490 BC. The Athenian general Miltiades surrounds the Persians on the plain at Marathon. Although heavily outnumbered, the Athenians kill 6400 Persians for the loss of only 192 Greeks.

Thermopylae, 480 BC. Xerxes makes up his mind to avenge the defeat at Marathon. His army, 300,000 strong, invades Greece from the north-east, supported by 800 triremes. Athens forms a league of Greek cities, commanding the navy and persuading Sparta to lead the land forces. The Persians advance towards Athens; Leonidas of Sparta occupies the narrow pass at Thermopylae with 7000 men. For two days he holds off attacks at odds of 40 to 1; but traitors lead Persian troops through secret mountain passes to surround him. The Persians march on to take Athens.

Salamis, 480 BC. Themistocles has led the population of Athens to the island of Salamis. He gathers a fleet of 300 ships. By sending a false message that the Greek fleet has decided to escape, Themistocles lures the enormous Persian fleet into the treacherous waters of the narrow Salamis channel. The Greeks scatter the enemy and sink large numbers of ships. The scattered Persian fleet heads for home.

Below: A battle between Spartans and Argives. The Spartans are on the right. Some of the soldiers are wearing the bell cuirass of bronze. Others wear a lighter tunic made from layer upon layer of linen stuck together. Most of the soldiers are wearing the Corinthian type of helmet. This was made of bronze and covered the entire head but for the eyes, nose and mouth. It probably had a felt lining. Others are wearing the Chaldean type, with a more open face and uncovered ears. On the helmets are horsehair crests.

The Spartans

The men of Sparta were trained as soldiers from their early youth. Their bravery was renowned; so were the hard conditions in which they lived. But while Sparta was a state ruled by soldiers, the soldiers were ruled by fear.

From the moment a Spartan boy was born, he had a single destiny – to be a soldier. State officials examined each baby to make sure it was healthy. Weak or sickly infants were taken to the mountains and left to die. Healthy boys were taken from their mothers at the age of seven and sent to a junior military school. Here they lived a tough life, concentrating on sports training, until they were old enough to join the army. A Spartan could marry at 20, but he still had to eat, live, and sleep at his regimental barracks until he was 30. The barracks were uncomfortable and the food was bad. It included a "black broth" made of pork stock, vinegar, and salt. One comfort-loving Athenian said he was no longer surprised at the Spartans' courage, for surely a man would rather die than go on living that sort of life. We still use the word Spartan to describe hard living conditions.

This strange state of affairs had come about because the Spartan citizens depended for their food on a vast population of land-slaves called helots. A great rebellion by these slaves started in 640 BC and lasted for 20 years. This frightened the Spartans so much that they put all their energies into training a standing army which could control their slaves.

Life in Sparta was tough, disciplined, and by Athenian standards very dull. Sparta itself was not much more than a collection of country villages with wooden houses set in woods and fields. Spartan citizens were forbidden to work.

Left: This bronze figure of a warrior dates from the beginning of the 5th century BC. It probably shows a Spartan.

Right: A bronze statue of a running girl, thought to be Spartan. Spartan girls were trained as athletes to fit them to be the mothers of warriors. During their training they wore short skirts to help them run better.

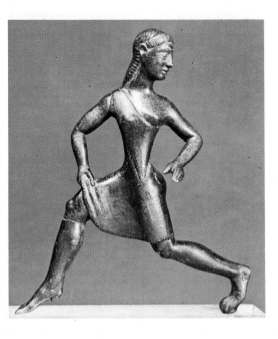

The Golden Age of Athens

The 400s saw the Golden Age of Athens – a time when it was the richest and most powerful city in Greece and the home of the greatest dramatists, artists, philosophers, and statesmen of the time.

Athens was at its greatest during the 400s BC. At this time its statesmen, soldiers, philosophers, writers, and artists achieved so much that this is often called the Golden Age of Greece. But this Golden Age was a short one. It lasted barely 60 years.

Athens was ruled by *democracy*. Any citizens could take part in the government of his city, and after 450 BC he was even paid by the state for doing so. Pericles thought that it was the glory of Athens that "power here is not in the hands of a minority, but of the whole people".

The city's governing body was the Assembly or *Ecclesia*. This met every nine days, and every citizen had the right to speak there. A council or *Boule* of 500 citizens, chosen by lot, met every day to prepare the business to go before the assembly. Committees ran the day-to-day business of the city. Each of these committees had ten members. They included inspectors of weights and measures, tax inspectors, police commissions, and street cleaning and safety committees. Only three dozen posts were filled by election, and these were positions, like military commands, where experience was essential.

There were no judges or lawyers in Athens. Instead, juries of 200 or 500

The Acropolis of Athens. The hill was a fortified citadel in Mycenaean times. The first Parthenon – the temple of Athene Parthenos, Athene the Virgin – was begun about 485 BC. It was destroyed by the invading Persians five years later. After the great Greek victory over the Persians, Pericles resolved to rebuild the Acropolis more magnificently than ever before. He used the finest architects and sculptors of the day to create a glittering complex of temples and statues. From left to right, along the top of the hill: the ceremonial gateway, the Propylea; the Erectheum; at its highest point, the Parthenon itself.

were selected by lot. When they had heard the case they voted by secret ballot to decide the guilt or innocence of the accused person.

To us, the most surprising thing about the system was that the people who made up the committees did not need to have any experience. But even Pericles said that he was sure that the simplest craftsman could understand all the responsibilities of citizenship.

Athens gains power

The rise of Athens started with the Greek victory over the Persians in 479. The Athenian navy played a very important part in this. As they pressed eastwards the Athenian warships freed many eastern Greek cities from Persian rule. With these and other eastern Greeks, Athens formed an alliance. It was called the Confederation of Delos, and its members gave ships or money to the headquarters on the sacred island of Delos in the Aegean.

Soon Athens was all-powerful in the Confederation. And Pericles used the Confederation money to beautify Athens. Under his direction the finest artists and sculptors in Greece worked on the temples and buildings of the Acropolis.

War breaks out

Naturally the other members of the Confederation were against their money being used to rebuild Athens. And they found themselves being treated more and more as slaves, rather than allies. Then, in 431, Athens went to war with Sparta and her allies who were threatening trade. Pericles persuaded the people from the surrounding countryside to come and camp within the Long Walls, which made a 5-mile (8-kilometer) corridor between Athens and its port, the Piraeus. This let the Spartans ravage the countryside, while the Athenian fleet was able to supply the people with food. Two years running, the Spartans invaded in spring, pillaging the land and easily defeating the Athenian army. The Athenian fleet sailed round the Peloponnese to attack Sparta and its allies. In the fall, the invaders were forced to return home for more supplies.

Then came total disaster. A terrible epidemic of plague broke out among all the peasants cooped up between the Walls. About a quarter of the population died – including Pericles himself. The war dragged on. Athens lost several chances to make peace by making greedy demands. Peace was made in 421 BC but then Athens sent an expedition to attack Syracuse, a powerful city in Sicily. It was a complete failure. War went on until Athens' last great fleet was destroyed in 404 and, after a siege, the starving city surrendered to the Spartans.

Marble bust of Pericles, a Roman copy of a portrait by the Cretan sculptor Cresilas. The face is calm and rather aloof – a clear effort to show Pericles more as a god than a man. Pericles's helmet is pushed back. (Some historians say that Pericles, who had a slightly misshapen head, preferred to be shown wearing a helmet.) Such a portrait firmly links Pericles with the ancient heroes of Greek legend. This makes it easier to understand how some of his fellow-citizens were suspicious of him, and accused him of a secret wish to become Tyrant of Athens.

Works from the three ages of Greek sculpture. Left: A girl, perhaps a goddess, from the 6th century BC – the Archaic period. She stands stiffly, her mouth curved into a mysterious smile. Traces of paint show that the Greeks used to paint their statues. Below: A fragment of the Parthenon frieze, showing a man tying his sandals. This carving, by Phidias, comes from the Classical period. Above: Hermes with the child Dionysus by the 4th-century sculptor Praxitiles. By this time, Greek taste was turning towards a soft romantic style.

The citizens of Athens were divided into three classes for military service. The first were people with an annual income worth more than 300 measures of grain. Most of the old aristocratic Athenian families came into this class. They provided the cavalry, and the trierarchs who commanded the warships. The middle class, of citizens with an income worth more than 200 measures of grain, provided the foot-soldiers. Many of the lowest class served as oarsmen in the navy. All citizens between 18 and 59 could be called for military service.

Many professional teachers and thinkers came to Athens in the 5th century. Some of these, the *sophists*, taught public speaking to young men who wished to shine in politics and in the law-courts. Others were serious and original thinkers who found Athens the ideal place for talking about their ideas.

Among the most famous of these teachers was the philosopher Socrates (469–399 BC). He was accused of turning the youth of Athens against the gods, and he was made to commit suicide by drinking the poison hemlock. His greatest pupil Plato (c429–347) carried on his work. Plato founded a school in the grounds of the Akademia gymnasium. This school specialized in mathematics. One of Plato's pupils, Aristotle (384–322), founded another school, the Lyceum, which taught philosophy. Aristotle himself went on to Macedonia where he was tutor to the king's son, Alexander – whom we know as Alexander the Great.

Everyday Life

Daily life in Greece varied little from state to state. On the whole it was simple, with few luxuries. Strange to us are the time spent in the gymnasia, and the part played by slaves.

Around the splendid public buildings of a Greek city clustered the houses of the citizens. These were made of mudbrick on a stone foundation. The average citizen lived in a house about 60 feet (18 meters) square. The ground floor rooms were grouped round a central courtyard, overlooked on three sides by the upper story. These houses were usually grouped together. But a rich man might have a house in its own grounds.

The father, as head of the family, was responsible for his wife, his children, and his household slaves – all of whom lived in his house. The senior member of the family was responsible for his parents and other branches of the family as far as second cousins. This strong sense of family reached back to include dead ancestors, whose graves were carefully tended.

Daily routine

The day began early for all citizens. At sunrise they had a light breakfast. Craftsmen would start work at once in their shops, which were often part of their houses. Businessmen went to the agora, the meeting place which was the hub of the city's business affairs. Back at home, the women and slaves would be busy with household tasks. Slaves did the cleaning and cooking, fetched water from the well, took the children to school, and went off to market to buy provisions. The citizen's wife took part in the cooking, and wove cloth for the family's clothes. Women stayed very much in the background. Girls were taught separately from boys, and had little education. Marriages were arranged by the families.

An important part of the citizen's day was the time he spent at the gymnasium. He exercised in the sand-covered, open-air *palaistrum*. Then he had a bath, and he rubbed down his body with scented oils. In the baths, and in the covered

Terracotta figure of a young girl playing a lyre. Greek music was played at religious festivals, athletic games, and dinner parties. A well-educated citizen was expected to play an instrument.

SLAVERY

Slavery had existed in Greece since the remote past, and was too long-established and too useful for the Greeks ever seriously to question it. Slaves worked in the house, in workshops and factories, and in the mines. They taught small children to read and write.

Most slaves were prisoners of war, sold first to slave dealers who in turn sold them in the city marketplaces. Many of them were non-Greek "barbarians" (a term the Greeks applied to all those who spoke another language, making "ba-ba" sounds). But Greeks were quite prepared to sell fellow-Greeks into slavery as well.

Slaves, of course, had no political rights; they could not vote or hold office. But they did not have to do military service and, in Athens at least, were protected by law against ill-treatment.

Above all, the Greeks thought of slavery as a way of leaving the citizen time to do the really important things of life — to serve in the Assembly, on a jury, or on any of the committees by which his city was governed.

Left: A slave accompanies his master on a walk through the streets.

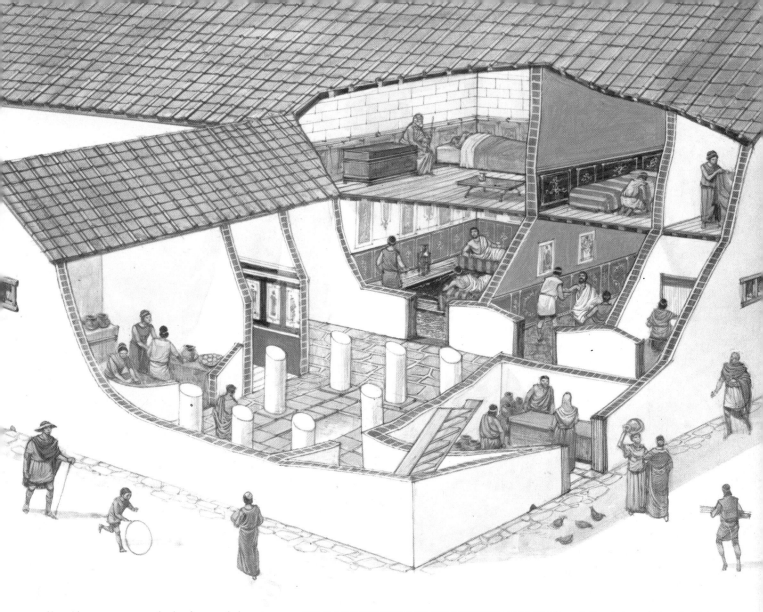

walks that surrounded the palaistrum, the citizens discussed everything from politics to art and philosophy. One of the most famous schools of philosophy in Athens – Aristotle's Lyceum – started as a series of open-air lectures and discussions in a gymnasium owned by a man called Lyceus.

In the evening came the main meal of the day, eaten around sunset. Food was brought in by slaves, and wealthy men sometimes hired singers and dancing girls for entertainment. Some of the guests might play or sing, or recite poetry. The Greeks loved meeting over a meal and discussing all manner of things. They even had dining "clubs", the members of which brought their own provisions in a basket.

The food eaten by the ancient Greeks sounds very dull to us. It was based on wheat and barley. Sometimes the grain was soaked in water and made into a paste mixed with flax-seed oil, salt, and coriander. It could also be ground in a hand-mill and baked into flat bread.

For hundreds of years there was little difference between the food of the poor and that of the rich. A poor man would eat olives, dried figs, and goat's milk cheese, with salt fish as a special treat. Richer people could afford fresh fish and small game such as deer, hare, partridge, and thrushes. The peasant washed down his food with water or goat's milk, while the rich drank wine (usually mixed with water in a *krater*, or mixing bowl).

A Greek town house built in the 5th century. The entrance from the street is hidden on the left; it leads through a passage into an open courtyard. On the right is a shop, opening on to the street. Part of the house is given over to women's rooms. These include a sitting-room and the kitchen. The citizen's wife worked with the female house-slaves, grinding corn for bread, weaving cloth on a loom, and cooking food. The main room in the house is the dining room, with four or five couches, and small three-legged tables.

Left: A Greek traveler. He wears a felt hat, a woolen cloak, and leather sandals fastened with thongs. Even wealthy Greeks traveled by foot.

Below: The neck of a vase from Attica, the countryside around Athens. It shows an Athenian girl being dressed by a slave. Above the girl hangs a mirror of polished bronze. Another slave brings a box, perhaps holding cosmetics.

DRESS

The basic Greek garment was called a *chiton*. It was made by pinning or sewing together two rectangular pieces of linen or muslin leaving holes for the head and arms. The loose, flowing tunic was then gathered at the waist. Chitons were often dyed — saffron yellow and red were favorite colors. Men's and women's chitons were made in the same way but women's were longer and fuller than those worn by men.

Both men and women wore an over-mantle called a *himation*. This was a plain oblong of woolen cloth with decorated borders.

Most Greeks — even wealthy ones — traveled on foot. Horses were expensive to rear and feed, and though they were fast they were uncomfortable to ride since the Greeks had no stirrups. Neither had they invented efficient harness, so heavy loads were carried in carts drawn by strong but slow oxen. Only the very rich could afford a light carriage, drawn by two horses, but women sometimes traveled in little donkey carts.

Wheeled vehicles had to have roads; but these were narrow and only roughly paved, especially over the steep mountain passes. Along the roads were inns and shops for the travelers — comedy writers made jokes about cheating innkeepers.

The tombstone of an Athenian doctor. The boy may be a patient.

The Greeks thought health was the greatest gift of the gods to men. They spent a great deal of time on keeping their bodies strong and healthy. Early doctors gave advice on diet and exercise, and cured the sick with old remedies. Sick people made pilgrimages to temples of the god Asclepios.

But there were doctors who were far more scientific. Patients were questioned about every aspect of their lives. Only when every scrap of information had been written down did the doctor begin a cure. Even then, different medicines were carefully tested and their effects were noted too. The first medical textbooks were written by Hippocrates of Cos (479–399 BC), the greatest doctor of his day. He set out the methods a doctor must follow: thorough investigation and careful observation. The scientific approach which is described in his books has remained the basis of medical practice until today.

EDUCATION

A Greek school had 60 to 100 pupils — all boys. They probably started pretty early in the morning, about 7 am. From the age of six or so, a boy would be led off to school by a family slave. He learned to read and write, to play on the double flute (*aulos*) and on the lyre. A great part of his schooling was sports training. The sons of wealthy parents went on after their ordinary schooling to attend the lectures of traveling teachers called sophists (from the Greek word *sophia*, meaning wisdom).

An Athenian boy at school, from a 5th-century vase. He is shown practising the lyre under the eye of his teacher. To the right he is being given a reading lesson.

MONEY

The earliest Greek money was in the form of bronze tripods, basins, axes, rings, and spits. From the 9th century onwards, iron spits called *obelos* were used as the basic unit of currency. Sparta continued to use this clumsy system of money long after the rest of Greece had begun to use coin money. This probably began in the kingdom of Lydia and spread first to the trading cities of Asia Minor and then to Greece itself. Many cities started to issue their own coinage — pieces of gold, silver, and electrum (a mixture of gold and silver) stamped with the symbol of the city.

At first these coins were too valuable for everyday use, but soon a system of smaller silver coins developed. They were used for everyday trading in the marketplace. The system was so useful that coins of smaller value still were made — this time from bronze.

The smallest unit of currency was the *obol*. Six of these made one *drachma*; a hundred drachmas made a *mina*; and sixty minae made up one *talent*. The *stater* was worth about two drachmas.

Stamped coinage was imported into the Greek world from Asia Minor. Left: An electrum stater from Phrygia. Electrum is an alloy of gold and silver. Below left: A 4-drachmae silver piece from Athens, stamped with an owl, the symbol of Athene. Such pieces were made between 527 and 430 BC. Bottom left: A beautiful silver 10 drachmae piece from Syracuse. It is stamped with the head of the nymph Arethusa.

Below: An Athenian carved relief of the early 5th century BC, showing a game very similar to hockey.

Festivals

The Greeks had no weekend holidays. Instead each month had a festival – a welcome break from work and a time for feasting and fun as well as worship.

Today we take it for granted that everyone has at least one day off a week. But the ancient Greeks had no regular weekend holidays. Instead the various months of the year were marked by religious festivals. These must have been a welcome break. Not only did work stop during the festival, but those taking part were able to eat the cooked meat that had been prepared for the god or goddess. For meat was a luxury in the Greek world.

But festivals meant more than just having a good time. They were based on the belief that man had a duty to discover the correct way of showing respect to the gods. Each shrine had its proper sacrifices and ceremonies. Some of these ceremonies were always just local affairs, but others grew in importance to become major festivals which drew visitors from every part of the Greek world. Among these were the Olympic Games.

One of the most important Greek festivals was the Panathenea, held in Athens in the Greek month of Hekatombion (July/August). During this festival the wooden statue of the goddess Athene in the Acropolis was brought a magnificent new robe woven by the women of the city. The robe was first taken in procession from Athens to the temple of Demeter at Eleusis, and then back to the Acropolis. At the head of the procession were the *kanephoroi* or basket-bearers. These were women, dressed in richly embroidered robes. They carried gold and silver dishes on which were garlands of flowers, the first fruits of the harvest, and the sacred knife for sacrificing cattle to Athene. Behind the kanephoroi came the hundred cattle doomed to die.

When the procession at last reached the altar of Athene, the cattle were solemnly slaughtered and cooked. The meat was passed to the citizens to eat. This yearly festival was celebrated with particular magnificence every fourth year, when it was called the Great Panathenea. In 566 BC came the foundation of the Panathenaic Games, on the pattern of the Olympic Games. Victorious athletes were given vases full of the finest olive oil – for the goddess Athene had given men the olive tree.

The festivals and mysteries continued even after Greece was in Roman hands.

A Greek sacrifice in about 550 BC. The priest prepares the altar while his young assistant holds the sheep to be sacrificed. Behind them in procession walk musicians and girls. All wear ceremonial robes and garlands. This plaque, painted on wood, was dedicated to nymphs at a shrine near Corinth.

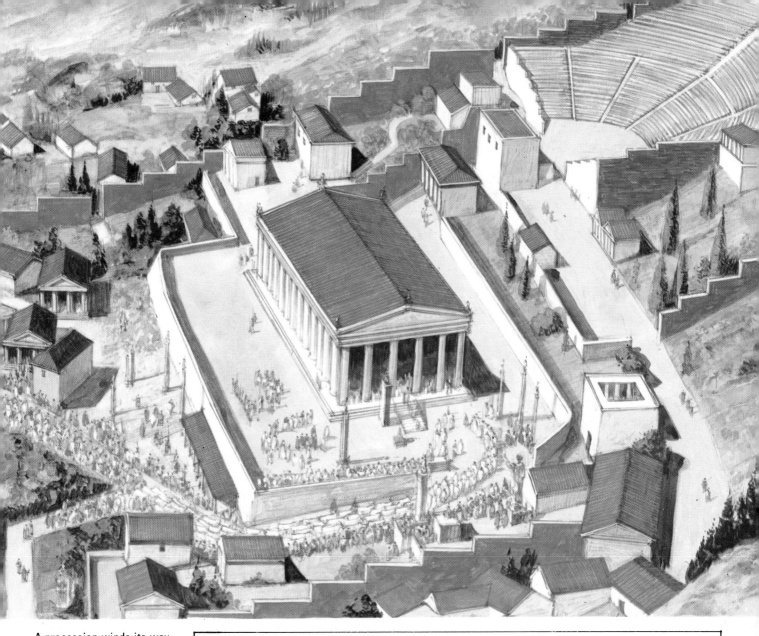

A procession winds its way up to the Temple of Apollo at Delphi. The Greek city states vied with one another to donate buildings and treasure to Delphi, in an attempt to win the favor of the Oracle of Apollo. Despite its riches, Delphi had no army, for the priests believed that Apollo would never allow his sanctuary to be defiled by an invader.

The Greek year ran from midsummer to midsummer. These were the main festivals at Athens.

Greek month	English equivalent	Festival	Deity honored
Skirophorion	June/July	Arrephoroi	Athene
		Dipoleia	Zeus
		Diisoteria	Zeus and Athene
Hekatombion	July/August	Panathenea	Athene
Roedromion	September/October	Mysteries of Demeter	
Pyanopsion	October/November	Chalkeia or Feast of the smiths	Athene and Hephaestus
Maimakterion	November/December	Maimakteria	Zeus
Antihesteria	February/March	Lenaia	Dionysus
		Diasia	Zeus/Meilichios
Elaphebolion	March/April	Great Dionysia	Dionysus
Thargelion	May/June	Thargelia	Apollo and Artemis

There were many other minor festivals and celebrations scattered throughout the year. In the bean-boiling feast of the Pyanepsia, children carried poles wound with wool from door to door, receiving gifts of fruit, bread, cakes, and jars of oil and honey. The Haephestia, in honor of Hephaestus the blacksmith of the gods, was celebrated at night with a torchlight race between teams of runners.

The Theater

The theater was born in 6th-century Greece. Of the thousands of Greek plays written only a few remain, but these are so great that they are performed and studied today.

In the 6th century BC the worship of Dionysus, god of wine and fertility, became an official cult in Athens. All the citizens were expected to attend his spring festival, the Great Dionysia. At this festival masked dancers and singers acted out legends about Dionysus. And these rituals began to develop into the first plays.

At first there was no special building for performances – just a circular patch of beaten ground, the *orchestra*, with an altar to Dionysus in the center. Spectators sat around it in a ring of temporary wooden stands. These stands were put up for the occasion each year until 498 BC when they collapsed and killed several people. After this a permanent open-air theater was built near the temple of Dionysus.

The early Greek plays were more like religious ceremonies than modern plays. The actors sang or chanted the lines

There were three kinds of Greek play.

Tragedies had serious themes, often involving sacrifice; in classical Greek theater the individual had to sacrifice his own happiness for the common good.

Satyr plays were written by the tragic authors. These plays made fun of a legend, and the chorus was dressed as satyrs — men with animal characteristics, such as a horse's tail.

Comedies were boisterous and vulgar, poking fun equally at gods and men, with rough horseplay and sharp jokes. Even the best-known and respected citizens might be shown as fools and scoundrels.

A terracotta figure of a masked Greek actor. He is playing the part of a slave, or perhaps a peasant. Masks were made of stiffened linen, and sometimes had a small megaphone built into the mouth, to help the actor to project his voice. Masks allowed a Greek audience to identify what kind of character an actor was playing – a tragic hero, a god, or a comic slave.

After the 5th century BC, every major Greek city had its own theater, with ceremonial seats for important officials. These are in the theater of the Asian Greek city of Priene, in modern Turkey.

Right: The theater at Delphi, built in the 4th century BC. The first stone theaters were circular, with seats completely surrounding the central earth floor. Later the seats were arranged in a semicircle. Behind the orchestra was a building from which the actors came to the stage. Later still movable scenery was used, while complicated machinery behind the building was used for special effects. For thunder, pebbles were rolled on copper sheets. Mirrors were flashed for lightning. The theaters were so skilfully built that even people sitting right at the back could hear every word spoken by an actor.

Right: A reconstruction of a typical Greek theater.
Below: Four great Greek dramatists. Aeschylus (525–456 BC) wrote the first great tragedies. Sophocles and Euripides wrote tragedies in the later 5th century. Aristophanes (448–380 BC) wrote comedies.

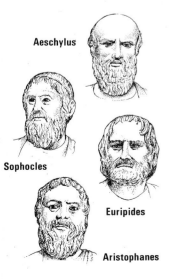

Aeschylus

Sophocles

Euripides

Aristophanes

THE GREAT DIONYSIA
The Great Dionysia in Athens became the occasion of an annual competition. Three writers each had to submit four plays (three tragedies and a satyr play). All the plays had as their theme some Greek myth or legend. In later times a comedy was performed on the last day of the festival. Judges had ceremonial seats, on which were inscribed their names, while priests from various temples also sat in the front row. In the center sat the priest of Dionysus, with the representative of Delphi on his right hand. After 449 BC there were prizes for actors as well as for the plays.

together, in a group or *chorus* about 50 strong. From time to time one actor separated himself from the group to describe events in the life of the hero. Later on the chorus became fewer, and there were up to three solo actors, playing as many as 15 different parts between them. There were no women; female parts were taken by men, and all the actors wore masks.

Violence was never shown on the Greek stage. Instead an eyewitness gave a description of events, and the bodies of the dead might be carried on to the stage. These would be played by "extras" or dummies; the speaking actors were too valuable to spare. Emblems were used to make sure that people knew who the characters were. Zeus carried a thunderbolt, Artemis a bow, and Poseidon a trident. A king held a scepter and a warrior a sword, while a traveler wore a broad-brimmed hat and a herald wore a wreath.

From Athens the Greek love of drama spread out until all the important cities had a theater. Eventually touring companies of actors traveled all over the Greek world.

The Games

Every four years heralds proclaimed a Sacred Truce for the Olympic Games, held in honor of the god Zeus. The Greeks valued fitness very highly, and successful athletes won respect and fame.

The Greeks thought it was very important to develop their bodies to be as fit and strong as possible. In every Greek city boys were encouraged to spend as much time as they could exercising in the gymnasium under the watchful eye of an instructor. In Sparta, this part of a boy's education was thought much more important than learning to read and write! And the reward for the best athletes was to take part in one of the great athletic festivals, or Games.

All over Greece there were regular athletic festivals. Some of these Games grew from small local affairs into international events attended by people from all over the Greek-speaking world. These great festivals were thought so sacred that even states at war would call a truce in order to be able to compete.

Left: The gymnasium at Olympia, where the athletes trained. On its walls were inscribed the names of athletes of the past. The round objects are baths where the athletes were splashed with water.

Right: The discus thrower – a Roman copy of a bronze statue made by the sculptor Myron, in about 450 BC. Throwing the discus – a flat bronze plate – was one of the sports in the pentathlon. The pentathlon was the most important event of the Olympics, because the Greeks admired all-round excellence above everything.

DELPHI AND THE PYTHIAN GAMES

The stadium at Delphi was built in the mid-5th century BC. The stone seats were added later, and could hold 17,000 people. Near one end was a fountain where spectators could drink. The stadium lies high on the mountainside, above the temple and the theater.

The Pythian Games, held here every four years, were second only to the Olympics in importance. They were sacred to Apollo, and opened with a hymn to the god, accompanied by a lyre. The athletic program was much the same as at Olympia. There were also a long-distance race for boys and a race for athletes clad in full bronze armor. A great difference was the importance of music; there were competitions for singers and lyre and flute players.

The stadium at Delphi, built about 450 BC.

The Olympics

Greatest of all were the Olympic Games. They were held in honor of Zeus every four years from 776 BC to AD 393 – 1168 years. They were held at the time of the August full moon, when the grain harvest had been gathered and there was a lull before the grape and olive harvest. Earlier in the year heralds went far and wide to announce the Games. They also announced that there would be no war until the Games were over. Athletes and spectators traveled from every part of the Greek world – from colonies in the Black Sea, from cities of Asia Minor, from the Aegean islands. The contestants spent a month training at the nearby town of Elis. Then they assembled at the Temple of Zeus with their trainers and fathers, and took a solemn oath to compete honorably.

On the first morning of the Games were horse races and a four-horse chariot event; in the afternoon came the five *pentathlon* events – sprint, long-jump, discus, javelin, and wrestling. Elegance of performance was thought very important. The next day was the day of the full moon and was sacred to Zeus. There were no contests; the crowd of some 60,000 spectators and contestants gathered around the altar of Zeus. Then a grand parade of officials, athletes, and delegates from the competing cities brought their offerings to the gods. On the final day running races were held in the morning, while the afternoon was given over to boxing, wrestling, and a no-holds-barred contest called the *pancration* in which some contestants even lost their lives.

The winning athletes were given only simple wreaths of olive leaves. But when they got back to their native cities they could expect a hero's welcome.

Two scenes from vases, showing competitors in the Games. Above: The pancration, a combination of boxing and wrestling. Serious injuries were common.
Below: A boxing match. Boxers' fists were bound with strips of heavy leather.

37

Philip and Alexander

From a semi-barbarian kingdom in the north came a father and son who were to reshape the ancient world. Philip of Macedon and his son Alexander united strife-torn Greece behind them, then turned to wider horizons.

A battle scene from the so-called "Alexander sarcophagus" from the city of Tyre. The panels are carved with scenes from Alexander's conquest of Persia. In this detail Greek warriors are fighting Persians. In Greek art, Greek soldiers are usually shown fighting naked, with their helmets pushed back. The Persian fashion of wearing pants was laughed at by Greeks for centuries.

The long-drawn-out Peloponnesian War between the Greek states ended with the defeat of Athens and the Spartans in control. But the Spartans were harsh rulers. Alliances grew up against them and the city of Thebes became more powerful. Under their brilliant general Epaminondas the Thebens savagely defeated the Spartans at the battle of Leuctra in 371 BC.

Soon after this a young Macedonian, Philip, spent three years as a hostage in Thebes. He greatly admired Epaminondas; and probably was inspired by him to reorganize the Macedonian army when he became ruler some ten years later. Although the royal house of Macedon was Greek-speaking, the kingdom was semi-barbarian. Philip started by defeating the tribes of Macedonia. Then he turned south, and gradually gained control of the city states. Thebes, pleased when he defeated their enemy neighbors, held aloof until too late. Athens was busy with revolts among its allies. In 339 BC Philip defeated a combined Theban-Athenian army and became master of Greece.

Philip now decided to invade the weak but fabulously rich Persian Empire. He was elected supreme general of all the Greeks. But at this vital moment Philip was assassinated. Immediately revolts broke out all round, but they were soon put down by his son, Alexander.

Into action

Alexander was only 20 but he showed at once that he had all the military genius of his father. He put down the revolt firmly. He made an example of Thebes, killing

	Empire of Alexander
	Dependent states
	Cities founded by Alexander

MACEDONIA

BLACK SEA

CASPIAN SEA

Thebes

Kodjend

Samarkand

MEDITERRANEAN SEA

Alexandria

Alexandropolis

Alexandria

Alexandria

Nicephorium

Gaugamela

N

Damascus

Bucep

R. Indus

Babylon

Susa

Alexandria

Alexandria

Memphis

Alexandria

Persepolis

Alexandria

R. Nile

Alexandria

RED SEA

Alexandria

some 600 of its inhabitants, and laying waste the city. This ruthless action brought the other Greek cities into line. Like his father, Alexander was able to unite a Greek and Macedonian army under his leadership, and in 344 BC he invaded the Persian Empire.

One after another the Persian cities of Asia Minor fell to Alexander. Marching into Egypt, he defeated its Persian overlords and was crowned king. He finally defeated the Persians at Gaugamela in 331 BC. Next he pressed eastwards as far as northern India. Here, at last he had to halt; his war-weary army would go no farther. He returned to Persia and in 323, while in Babylon, he died of a fever – or possibly of poison.

Philip and Alexander were both outstanding generals, and recklessly brave. Both men were able to command the loyalty of even the toughest soldiers. Alexander was only 32 when he died, but he was master of the greatest empire the world had known.

Alexander the Great's empire about 325 BC. His 10 years of fighting left him master of territory from the Mediterranean to India. He led his 40,000 Macedonians on a journey of over 5000 miles (8000 kilometers).

The 23-year-old Alexander leads the charge against the Persians at the battle of Issus (333 BC). This is a detail from a huge mosaic discovered at Pompeii – a copy of a lost Greek painting of about 300.

The Legacy

When Alexander died his empire was divided. But it remained Greek in thought and feeling. In the new Greek city of Alexandria in Egypt, learning flourished as never before.

The three centuries between the death of Alexander and the Roman conquest of the Near East are usually called the Hellenistic Age. In ten years, Alexander had conquered the greatest empire that the world had ever seen. Greek language and Greek culture now stretched from the Mediterranean to India.

But Alexander died before he could organize his new empire properly. His generals said that on his death-bed he left his empire "to the strongest", and a struggle broke out between them as to who should control it. After years of senseless warfare a new map of the world emerged. In Egypt and southern Syria ruled Ptolemy I. In Asia, the family of Alexander's general Seleucus held sway from the Aegean to India. In Macedonia, Alexander's own homeland, years of civil war was ended by Antigonus Gonatas, who swiftly extended his power over the mainland Greek cities.

Under these powerful and wealthy monarchs, art, architecture, science and city planning were greater than ever before. At least 60 new cities were built in Asia.

Ruins of Ephesus, in Asia Minor (modern Turkey). Ephesus was an ancient Ionian Greek city, a wealthy seaport with a famous Temple of Artemis – one of the Seven Wonders of the World. Ephesus twice fell victim to the Persian empire, but was liberated by Alexander in 333 BC. After Alexander's death, his empire was divided between his generals. Under them the eastern Greek cities rose in renewed splendor. They lavished their wealth on magnificent temples and public buildings. Ephesus prospered long into Roman times.

Alexandria

The greatest of all the Hellenistic cities was Alexandria in Egypt. It was founded by Alexander the Great in 322 BC. His successor in Egypt, Ptolemy, made Alexandria his capital. Ptolemy extended the harbor and built the Pharos lighthouse, a 400-foot (122-meter) tower which was one of the seven wonders of the world.

Alexandria became a great naval base and trading port – the largest and richest Greek city in the world. Poets, writers, philosophers, and scientists came there. The library contained 700 volumes.

Here enormous advances were made in every field of knowledge. Eristratos the physician and his rival Herophilos investigated the anatomy of the human body, and discovered the principle of the circulation of the blood. Euclid wrote a 30-volume instruction book on geometry that was used until the 19th century AD. Eratosthenes showed that the world was round. Ctesibios, Archimedes, and Hero invented pumps, pulleys, screw-cutting machines, and even steam turbines. At its greatest, Alexandrian science reached a point that was not matched until the 17th century.

Right: Alexander's conquests in India had a lasting effect. Long after Greek rule had waned, Indian sculptors in Gandhara (north-west India) were carving sculpture influenced by Hellenistic styles.

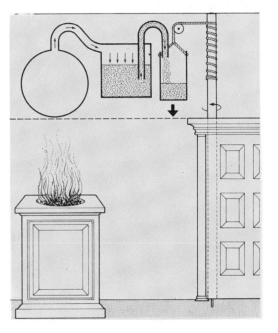

Hero of Alexandria's machine for opening a temple door (3rd century BC). When the air in the flask was heated, it expanded and pushed down the water in the tank, forcing it through a pipe into a suspended cistern. When enough water had flowed into the cistern, it sank to the ground, turning the door post to which it was attached by a rope.

The Aphrodite of Rhodes, about 2nd century BC. The sculptors of the Hellenistic period were fascinated by smooth, flowing forms – in contrast to the severe styles of the Classical Age.

The expanding world

This was an age in which every educated man, wherever he was born, spoke and wrote Greek. At centers of learning like Syracuse and Alexandria amazing advances were made in mathematics, geography, engineering, and medicine. Greek travelers voyaged across the Atlantic to Britain and Norway, explored the coasts of Africa, and sailed to India.

But the old Greek ideals of responsible citizenship grew less. The Hellenistic kings ruled through governors and powerful armies. Throughout the Hellenistic world the rich got richer, while the poor grew steadily poorer.

Glossary

Acropolis A fortified citadel built on high ground to protect the city. The most famous acropolis in ancient Greece was that of Athens.

Agora The marketplace of a Greek city. It was a large open space surrounded by public buildings and temples.

Amphora A large clay pot, with two handles at the neck, used to store liquids such as wine or olive oil.

Archon One of the nine ruling magistrates of Athens. Archons were selected by lot to serve for one year. They supervised the law-courts and public religious ceremonies.

Areopagus A hill in Athens, sacred to Ares, god of war. Later, the name was given to the council which met on the hill to judge cases of murder.

Black-figure A method of decorating pottery, very common in Athens. The design was painted in black silhouette over the natural red of the clay.

Boule The council, made up of 500 citizens, which governed Athens. The Boule prepared laws which were then passed on to the Ecclesia for the approval of the people. It also made sure that the laws were kept.

Capital The carved top of a stone column. The three main types of Greek columns were the Doric, Ionic, and Corinthian orders.

Cella The part of a Greek temple in which the statue of the god stood. The entrance to the cella always faced to the east.

Chiton A Greek tunic of wool or linen worn by men and women alike. It was made of two lengths of material pinned or sewn together at the shoulders and gathered at the waist. Women's chitons were always long; those worn by men might be long or short.

Crater (krater) A pottery bowl, in which the Greeks mixed water and wine.

Demes (demoi) All of Attica was divided into small parishes, called demes. A deme numbered between 600 and 1200 citizens. It sent representatives to the Boule and provided soldiers for the army. When the son of a citizen reached his eighteenth birthday, his name was entered on the voting roll of his deme. In this way he was officially made a citizen.

Democratia Literally, "rule by the people". In Athens, this meant that all citizens had an equal right to take part in government. Also, no law could be passed without the approval of the Ecclesia, to which every citizen over the age of 20 belonged.

Ecclesia The assembly of the Athenian people. It met regularly on the Pnyx, a low hill to the west of the Acropolis. All citizens over the age of 20 were automatically members. Although the day-to-day running of Athens was left to the Boule, the final decision on any issue rested with the vote of the Ecclesia.

Elgin marbles Fragments of the ruined Parthenon, brought back to England by the Earl of Elgin (1766–1841). They are now in the British Museum.

Frieze A band of stonework running along the sides of a Greek building, between the tops of the columns and the roofline. It was often decorated with sculptures.

GREEK ARCHITECTURAL ORDERS

Doric

Ionic

Corinthian

There were two main styles of Greek architecture, the Doric and the Ionian. The Doric style, or order, was severe and simple. In a Doric temple the columns rose straight from the floor to a simple capital. The Doric order was really a stone version of the thatched wooden temples of the early Greeks. In those, wooden columns supported wooden cross-beams.

The Ionian order, as its name suggests, first came from the Greek cities of Asia Minor. It was a more delicate and decorative style than the Doric. The columns were taller and slimmer: at the base was a decorated plinth, at the top a carved, scrolled capital.

From the 5th century BC onwards, a new style, the Corinthian order, became popular. In it the capital at the top of the pillar was decorated with scrolls and sprays of acanthus leaves.

Gerousia The council of advisers to the two kings of Sparta. It was made up of 28 citizens over 60.

Helots Spartan slaves bound to the land that they worked. A fixed proportion of their produce went to feed the Spartan citizens. Helots had no legal rights, and were punished by death if they tried to escape.

Herodotus of Halicarnassus (c484–425 BC) The first Greek historian. His history of the Persian wars was based on his own conversations with those who had fought in them.

Hesiod (c8th century BC) An early Greek poet from Ascra in Boeotia. He collected many legends about the origins of the gods and of the world in his poem *Theogeny*. Another poem, *Works and Days*, contains advice on farming and sea-faring.

Himation A woolen cloak.

Homer The earliest known Greek poet. He probably lived in Asia Minor about 800 BC. His only known works are two epic poems, *The Iliad* and *The Odyssey*.

Hoplite The typical citizen-soldier of a Greek city state. Athenians were liable for military service between the ages of 18 and 60. A middle-class citizen equipped himself at his own expense as a foot-soldier. His helmet, breastplate, leg-guards, and shield were of bronze. His short sword was of iron, and he carried a 9-ft (3-meter) long spear.

Ionia A group of Greek cities on the coast of Asia Minor. Their inhabitants spoke the Ionian dialect of Greek. The cities, which included Chios, Ephesus, Miletus, and Samos, created the first flowering of Greek poetry, philosophy, and science.

Megaron The main room in the simple, rectangular houses of early Greek chiefs. In the center of the room was an open hearth, used for cooking and for religious ceremonies. The design became the basis of the Greek temple.

Oracles Places at which, as the Greeks believed, the gods spoke directly to men. The most famous oracle was that of Apollo at Delphi. Here the god "spoke" through the mouth of a priestess, while she herself was in a trance. The Greeks believed very seriously in oracles, and cities regularly sent ambassadors to Delphi to ask the advice of Apollo.

Peplos A woolen robe for women, made from a single length of cloth about 6½ ft by 10 ft (2 meters by 3 meters). It could be worn in several different ways, the simplest being to pin it at the shoulder leaving the right-hand side open. Every year, at the Panathenea, a richly decorated peplos was carried in procession to the statue of Athene on the Acropolis. Then the peplos, which was made by the women of Athens, was presented to the goddess.

Phidias (b. c490 BC) A famous Athenian sculptor, painter, and metal-worker. A friend of Pericles (see page 26), Phidias designed the sculpture of the Parthenon. Some of this — the famous Elgin Marbles — is now in the British Museum, London. In his own time, Phidias was best known for two colossal bronze and ivory statues. The first, the great figure of Athene in the Parthenon, was finished about 438 BC. The second, the statue of Zeus at Olympia, was complete by 430 BC. The workshops where Phidias prepared and cast his Zeus have been discovered at Olympia.

Praxitiles (d. c320 BC) Another great Athenian sculptor. He was especially admired for the elegance and beauty of his works. His statues of gods and goddesses portrayed them as young and graceful, not

This red-figure vase shows a Greek youth having a riding lesson. Such scenes from vases have helped historians find out about the everyday life of the ancient Greeks.

stern and severe, as earlier sculptors had done.

Pythia The priestess of Apollo at Delphi. At the time of its greatest fame there were three Pythias at Delphi to deal with the stream of those who had come to consult the oracle. During the ceremony, the Pythia, seated on a sacred bronze three-legged stool, entered a trance. While in her trance she spoke the words that the god had supposedly put into her mouth. These words, often confused, were written down by the temple priests, who then turned them into an answer to deliver to those who had come to ask the advice of the oracle.

Red-figure A 5th-century BC method of decorating pottery. Figures were left in the natural red of the clay, while the background was filled in with solid black.

Sarcophagus A container for a body, made of stone or terra cotta and usually shaped like a rectangular box. The outside was often decorated with paintings or relief carvings and inscriptions.

Stele A stone slab, often irregular in shape, which was set up as a marker. The best known are those put up over graves, which are often beautifully carved. They were also used as boundary stones.

Bold entries indicate a major mention.
Italic numerals indicate an illustration.

ACKNOWLEDGEMENTS

Photographs: Half title Michael Holford; contents page Ektodike, Athens (top), Ronald Sheridan (center), Zefa (bottom); page 7 Michael Holford (top), Louvre, Paris (bottom); 8, 9 Michael Holford; 11 Michael Holford (top); Ronald Sheridan (bottom); 12 Robert Harding Associates; 13 Lord William Taylour (center left), Michael Holford (right); 14 Ektodike, Athens; 15 Michael Holford (top and bottom), Ektodike, Athens (center); 16 British Museum (bottom right), Michael Holford; 17 Robert Harding Associates (top right), Ronald Sheridan (bottom left), Michael Holford (bottom right); 18 British Museum; 19 Ronald Sheridan (top), F. H. Birch/Sonia Halliday (center); 21 Michael Holford; 22 British Museum; 24 Waddington Collection (left), Michael Holford; 25 Zefa; 26 Michael Holford; 27 Ektodike, Athens (left and top right), Mansell Collection (bottom right); 28 Mansell Collection; 30 Michael Holford; 31 Mansell Collection (top right), Ronald Sheridan (bottom right), British Museum; 32 Phaidon; 34 Michael Holford (top), Sonia Halliday (bottom); 35 Sonia Halliday; 36 Michael Holford (left), Mansell Collection (right); 37 Robert Harding Associates (top), Michael Holford; 38, 39 Sonia Halliday; 40 Sonia Halliday; 41 Michael Holford (top), Ronald Sheridan (bottom); 43 Michael Holford.

Picture research: Jackie Cookson: Penny Warn.

	GREECE	*EUROPE*

BC 2000

2000-1900 Greek-speaking tribes arrive

2000 Stonehenge built in Britain

1650-1450 Mycenaeans grow in power

1500-1300 Bronze Age in northern Europe

1450 Cretan civilization destroyed

1220? Troy destroyed by expedition from mainland Greece

1150

1150 Dorians invade Greece. Collapse of Mycenaean civilization

1100s Phoenician colonies in Spain

900-750 Rise of city-states

900 Rise of Etruscans in Italy

776 Traditional date of first Olympic Games

750 Homer's Iliad and Odyssey composed

753 Traditional date of founding of Rome

700-500 Sparta dominates Peloponnese

600 Greeks found city of Massilia (now Marseilles) in France

507

507 Athenian democracy begins

509 Roman nobles drive out their Etruscan kings

490-479 Persian Wars

490 Common people of Rome rebel against nobles. They win some rights

477-405 Athens dominates the Aegean, and enjoys its Golden Age

450 Celtic La Tène culture develops

431-404 Peloponnesian War between Athens and Sparta

380 Celts attack Rome

356-338 Philip of Macedon makes himself master of Greece

336 Philip is murdered and his son Alexander succeeds him

336-323 Alexander wins an empire stretching from Egypt to north India

323

323 Alexander dies aged 32

NEAR EAST

EAST ASIA

2372-2255 Akkadian empire; founded by Sargon

2040-1633 Egypt's Middle Kingdom

1792-1750 Hammurabi rules Babylon

1567-1085 Egypt's New Kingdom

1450-1180 Hittite empire at its height

1200 Sea Peoples raid Mediterranean coasts

1150 Greeks begin to colonize coast of Asia Minor

973 Solomon becomes King of Israel

2500 Indus Valley civilization arises in India

1500 Indus Valley civilization falls to invaders

1500-1027 Shang dynasty in China

1027-256 Chou dynasty in China

587 Nebuchadrezzar of Babylon besieges Jerusalem

539 Persians conquer Babylonia

c 600 Early cities near river Ganges in India

563 Birth of the Buddha in India

551 Chinese sage Confucius born

533 Persians invade India

360s Revolts in Persian empire

334-332 Alexander the Great conquers the Persian empire

326 Alexander the Great invades north India